Y0-BOE-904

Lion

by Mary Hoffman

STECK-VAUGHN
C O M P A N Y
A Subsidiary of National Education Corporation

The lion is called the king of beasts.
Tigers are the only big cats larger than
lions. Lions can be four feet tall, ten feet
long, and weigh over 400 pounds.

Lion babies are called cubs. Cubs are born tiny and blind. Their faces and bodies have spots that help them hide in leaves when their mother is not with them.

Lions have two or three cubs per litter.
Cubs open their eyes after a week or two.
They drink milk for a few months.

The cubs can walk when they are three weeks old. They do not go far. Sometimes their mother carries them.

Lion fathers sometimes look after their cubs. Cubs can be very playful.

The mothers usually look after the cubs.
Mothers protect the cubs fiercely.

Other animals in the wild protect their young, too. African buffalo will even chase away lions.

Lionesses do most of the hunting. They are lighter and quicker than males. First lionesses hide, then they run and pounce.

Lions kill by biting the necks or breaking the backs of prey. They eat all they can.

Lions will hunt and eat together. Males
need over fifteen pounds of meat a day.

Lions strip away the meat with their sharp teeth. The male eats the most.

Lions sometimes go for days without meat. Usually they are able to find water.

Lions can sleep twenty or more hours a day. Cubs are more interested in food.

Male lions have dark hair on their heads and necks. The hair is called a mane.

Lions live in prides. Prides have two or more males, some females, and cubs. Prides have territories of over 65 square miles. Most lions live in East Africa. A few hundred live in India.

Lion cubs that are raised by people can grow to be very tame. They are easy to tame. But lions are wild animals. A lion looks more like the king of beasts when it is in the wild.

First Steck-Vaughn Edition 1992

First published in the United States 1985
by Raintree Publishers, A Division of Steck-Vaughn Company.

First published in the United Kingdom under the title
Animals in the Wild—Lion
by Belitha Press Ltd.
31 Newington Green, London N16 9PU
in association with Methuen Children's Books Ltd.

Dedicated to Ruth and Elizabeth.

Scientific Adviser: Dr. Gwynne Vevers, Picture Researcher: Stella Martin

Acknowledgments are due to Bruce Coleman Ltd for all photographs in
this book with the following exceptions:
Jacana Ltd pp. 4, 5, 8, 10, 16 and cover; Survival Anglia pp. 20 and 21.

Library of Congress number: 84-24794

Library of Congress Cataloging in Publication Data

Hoffman, Mary.
  Lion.

  (Animals in the wild)
  Summary: Describes a lion's life and struggles for survival in its natural
surroundings.
  1. Lions—Juvenile literature. [1. Lions]
I. Title. II. Series.
QL737.C23S48   1985   599.74'428   84-24794

ISBN 0-8172-2411-4   hardcover library binding

ISBN 0-8114-6881-X   softcover binding

4 5 6 7 8 9   95 94 93 92